Ezra's Book

Poetry from the Ezra Pound International Conference

Philadelphia, Pennsylvania, USA

June 2017

# The Ezra Pound Center for Literature
at the University of New Orleans

The Ezra Pound Center for Literature Book Series is a project dedicated to publishing a variety of scholarly and literary works relevant to Ezra Pound and Modernism, including new critical monographs on Pound and/or other Modernists, scholarly studies related to Pound and his legacy, edited collections of essays, volumes of original poetry, reissued books of importance to Pound scholarship, translations, and other works.

Series Editor: John Gery, University of New Orleans

Editorial Advisory Board

Barry Ahearn, Tulane University
Massimo Bacigalupo, University of Genoa
A. David Moody (Emeritus), University of York
Ira B. Nadel, University of British Columbia
Marjorie Perloff, University of Southern California
Tim Redman, University of Texas at Dallas
Richard Sieburth, New York University
Demetres P. Tryphonopoulos, Brandon University
Emily Mitchell Wallace, Bryn Mawr College

Also Available in the Ezra Pound Center for Literature Book Series

Catherine E. Paul, *Fascist Directive: Ezra Pound and Italian Cultural Nationalism*
Anderson Araujo, *A Companion to Ezra Pound's Guide to Kulchur*
Richard Parker, Editor, *Readings in The Cantos*, Volume 1
Catherine Paul and Justin Kishbaugh, Editors, *A Packet of Poems for Ezra Pound*
Massimo Bacigalupo, *Ezra Pound, Italy and the Cantos* (forthcoming)

This collection is dedicated to the memory of Gregory M. Harvey, whose continued support of and presence at the Ezra Pound International Conference was greatly appreciated and will be dearly missed.

Ezra's Book

POETRY FROM THE EZRA POUND INTERNATIONAL
CONFERENCE

PHILADELPHIA, PENNSYLVANIA, USA

JUNE 2017

EDITED BY JUSTIN KISHBAUGH &
CATHERINE E. PAUL

Copyright 2019 by Clemson University
ISBN 978-1-949979-19-0

Copyright 2019 Justin Kishbaugh and Catherine E. Paul (editorial matter and arrangement)

The copyright of individual contributions remains the copyright of the contributor.

Photos © Anderson Araujo, Walter Baumann, Galateia Demetriou, Justin Kishbaugh, Deric Nugmanov, Biljana D. Obradović, and Catherine E. Paul 2017

Editorial Assistants: Lindsey Cook, Kelley Gillis, Natalie Merrithew, Ely Middleton, Samantha Miller, Joy Sasnett, and Lauren Soash

Cover design by Lindsey Cook

To order copies, please visit the Clemson University Press website: www.clemson.edu/press/

Contents

Editors' Introduction • xi

Charles Bernstein • 1
   Swan Songs • 1
Eloisa Bressan • 6
   A Girl • 6
   Steps • 7
Andrei Bronnikov • 8
   Zen Elegies • 8
David Cappella • 13
   Urge/Surge • 13
   Nafplion Afternoon • 14
   Closing Time at the Ontological Hotel • 15
Mary de Rachewiltz • 17
   Poet on the BBC • 17
   For Katha • 18
   For Eva • 19
   Mesmerism • 21
   An Old Proverb • 23
Patrizia de Rachewiltz • 24
   The Blue-Stoned Bracelet • 24
   Did You Get My Little Sun? • 25
   In My Days and Nights • 26
   White Sails • 27
   Untitled • 28
   The Green Grotto • 29
Silvia Falsaperla • 30
   Beach Scene • 30
   The Piano • 32
   Leonardo Kaneshige • 34
J. Rhett Forman • 35
   Uncle Sam, the Repo Man • 35
   The Americaniad • 39
   Gold Rush • 40

John Gery • 41
    Descant on Pennsylvania • 41
    Suburban Prejudice • 43
    Ruffed Grouse • 46
    Decoy • 47
Jeff Grieneisen • 48
    On Our Thirteenth Anniversary • 48
    Sketch • 50
    The Ring • 51
Thomas Heffernan • 53
    Lines Written on Sept. 4, 2011 • 53
    Adam's Eve • 55
    Translator • 56
    Banker, Banking • 56
    A Different Banker • 57
    Billionaire • 57
    A Different Billionaire • 58
    Pilot • 59
    A Haibun • 60
    Haiku (untitled) • 60
Rodolfo Brandão de Proença Jaruga • 61
    Canto I • 61
Justin Kishbaugh • 64
    Black Water II • 64
    Keef Swagger • 66
    Serious Moonlight • 67
Mary Maxwell • 68
    Exercise • 68
    Ulysses in Hell: A Drama • 69
    Invocation • 73
Biljana D. Obradović • 75
    A Hierarchy of Names • 75
    Unlike My Happy Baby • 77
    She's Not a Hot Commodity Anymore • 78
    Mercury, "Friendship 7" • 79

Matthew Porto • 80
    A Whiff of Ambrosia • 80
    Way Station: Last Soirée • 82
Michele Reese • 83
    The Great French Wine Blight • 83
    Crop Insurance • 84
    Garnishes • 85
    Grape Pickers • 86
Ron Smith • 87
    Master • 87
    The Berth of Modern Poetry • 89
    Curse Tablet • 93

Photos of the Event • 95

Contributors • 109

Acknowledgments • 115

Editors' Introduction

We strove a little book to make for him . . .

With the title of *Ezra's Book*, this collection grows out of the poetry reading at the twenty-seventh Ezra Pound International Conference that took place June 19–23, 2017 at the Kislak Center for Special Collections, Rare Books and Manuscripts in the Van Pelt-Dietrich Library at the University of Pennsylvania. The reading, which served as the final presentational event, is a longstanding feature of the conference that supplements its scholarly activities with artistic productions that evidence and celebrate Pound's continued presence in and influence on the current practice of poetry and the poets producing it: "[T]here is a sense of his pounding, pounding (*Pounding*)" (*End* 8).

Occurring, as it did, in Pennsylvania, the conference took as its theme, "Ezra Pound, Philadelphia Genius, and Modern American Poetry," with the final two categories deliberately expanding to include the work and lives of Hilda Doolittle (H.D.), Marianne Moore, and William Carlos Williams. In turn, we, as editors of this collection, decided on the title, *Ezra's Book*, as an allusion to the small book of poems Pound wrote for H.D. while the two were still young, in love, and living in Pennsylvania. Of course, neither poet would remain in Pennsylvania or in a committed relationship with the other, but each would go on to become an accomplished poet, with Pound effectively creating Imagism and initiating Hilda's poetic career by pushing her into the pages of *Poetry* as the mysterious "H.D. Imagiste."

While the two poets would evolve beyond the boundaries of Imagism, its underlying craft of selecting, arranging, and directly treating subjective and objective particulars remained a constant feature of their work. Pound famously defined the "Image" as "that which presents an intellectual and emotional complex in an instant of time" and identified the "super-position"—or "one idea set on top of another"—as its basic structure ("A Few Don'ts" 200, "Vorticism" 286). Interestingly, Pound and H.D.'s relationship was seemingly most intense, as one might imagine, at its beginning and end, and Pound's volume of poems for H.D., *Hilda's Book*, and H.D.'s corresponding record of her relationship with Pound, *End to Torment*, together create a super-position of the relationship between the two poets, which, in no small way, took much of its shape from their Pennsylvania roots.

Pound wrote *Hilda's Book* between 1905 and 1907, which was, as H.D. remembers, "the time of [his] writing 'a sonnet a day when I brush my teeth'" (*End* 46). As Pound's first collection of poetry, *Hilda's Book* contains fifty-seven leaves and twenty-five poems that the young Pound wrote for H.D. while the prospect of their marriage was still a real possibility (to them at least). Pound bound the collection by hand in vellum and handwrote "Hilda's Book" on the cover in a stylized black script. Two of the poems are handwritten and the rest are typed in blue, though several contain handwritten corrections in black ink or red pencil. (*End* 67). Pound presented the book to H.D. in 1907, but it fell into the possession of Pound and H.D.'s mutual friend, Frances Gregg, who held on to it and kept it safe for years. Following the Nazi bombings of Plymouth in 1941 that unfortunately took Gregg's life, *Hilda's Book* was discovered among Gregg's possessions and eventually made its way into the collections at Harvard (Wilhelm 102). In a seemingly fated bit of symmetry or super-positioning, though, *Hilda's Book* remained unpublished until 1979, when it was printed at the end of H.D.'s *End to Torment*.

Although Pound's poems in *Hilda's Book* are imitative and bear the mark of their influences, they establish the life-long link for Pound between H.D. and trees that would lead him to nickname her "Dryad," a title that must have originated in the sylvan aspects of their Pennsylvania surroundings. "Ver Novum," for instance, begins with the line, "Thou that art sweeter than all orchards' breath" (*End* 71), and "Rendez-vous" concludes the collection with typically antiquated language that emphasizes H.D.'s "tree-born spirit of the wood" and how "[t]he moss-grown kindly trees … she could / As kindred claim" (84).

While the theme of trees continues throughout the book (including in the overtly titled poem "The Tree," that Pound would continue to include in subsequent collections of his poetry), Pound, at points, correlates his subject, H.D., with trees in ways that presage her later poetic manifestations for him. In "Domina," for example, Pound begins by calling her "tall and fair," likening her to "a poplar tree / When the wind bloweth merrily." And, in presenting H.D. as a tree and using a simile that refers to her eyes as "[n]ot clouded much to trouble me" (73), Pound seems to anticipate the lines in "Canto LXXXIII," in which, from the detention camp in Pisa, he remembers H.D., his Dryad, and her eyes: "Δρυάς, your eyes are like the clouds over Taishan / When some of the rain has fallen / And half remains yet to fall" (*Cantos* 544).

In another two poems in *Hilda's Book*, Pound also uses imagery that may have provided the later inspiration for H.D.'s Imagist effort, "Oread." More specifically, in "Green Harping," Pound creates a world in which his subject, who wears "violets in [her] leaf brown hair," is heralded by an "elfin horn" and crowned the elf queen of "Eringreen" (78). Then, in "Li Bel Chasteus," Pound mentions "the great green waves" and "rocky shore by Tintagoel" (80), which, if recalled or subconsciously super-positioned with the "elfin" world of "Green Harping," could certainly have acted as the origins of H.D.'s "Oread," in which the titular mountain nymph first encounters the sea and can only understand it in relation to the trees and rocks that make up her world: "Whirl up, sea— / whirl your pointed pines, / [. . .] cover us with your pools of fir" (*Collected* 55). Notably, "Oread" is the poem of H.D.'s that Pound would continue to recall and reprint. In fact, in his article "Vortex. Pound.," which appeared in the first installment of *Blast*, Pound offers "Oread" as the prime example of the poetic "IMAGE" (154).

When H.D. collected her journal entries recounting her relationship with Pound in *End to Torment*, the sylvan landscape of Pound's and her youth also seems to branch out through her memories. H.D. recalls the young Pound reading William Morris to her "in an orchard under blossoming—yes, they must have been blossoming—apple trees" (22), and, in particular, she remembers Pound literally running late for the last train to Wyncote because neither he nor she could force themselves to leave each other or their lovers' perch high in "the big maple tree in [the Doolittles'] garden." As he leaves, she laments, "Why had I ever come down out of that tree?" (12).

Like those of any native Pennsylvanian, H.D.'s memories of trees often lead to thoughts of winter, but, for the Imagist poet, those memories then lead to recollections of the "fiery kisses" from her first love that, like the young Pound himself, stood out from their surroundings. H.D. begins *End to Torment* with a description of Pound that clearly sets him both within and apart from the Pennsylvania winter. She imagines "[s]now on his beard," "[s]now blow[ing] down from the pine branches," and recalls their first kisses "[i]n the woods, in the winter" as "[e]lectric, magnetic" (3–4).

That scene and those kisses were of such an impact on H.D. that, as a coda for her *Helen in Egypt*, she includes a poem concerning her relationship with and feelings for Pound. She titles it "Winter Love," and that poem, too, seems to recall Pennsylvanian forests, with their "crisp leaves" and "a drift of snow / slid[ing] from a branch" (88). Thinly guised as a meeting between Helen and Odysseus (H.D.'s mother was named Helen, and Pound's father was named Homer), H.D. and Pound's relationship appears almost unadorned in "Winter Love." In the poem, we find Helen telling herself, "O, Helen, most blest, / recall first love and last" and then replaying an affair strikingly similar to the one wherein Pound broke his engagement with H.D. by sailing to Europe. She evokes his "tangled hair and beard" and his "wily undaunted look." She remembers his touch and her expectations of how she "expected completion" before hearing voices say of Pound/Odysseus "'he has gone, / he was only waiting for his Ship'" (96, 99).

In another fittingly super-positional maneuver, H.D. sent the completed "Winter Love" to Pound, telling him he might find it a "*divertissement*" to "slash it to pieces & return" (Korg 186). And, like the poetic Image itself, that invitation provides "that sense of freedom from time limits and space limits" ("A Few Don'ts" 200), which, as Jacob Korg also notes (186), recalls H.D.'s description in *End to Torment* of the original Imagist moment between her and Pound, in the British Museum tea room, when he declares her work "poetry" and renames her "H.D. Imagiste." ("A Few Don'ts" 200, Korg 186, *End* 18). Notably, those Imagist moments and his relationship with H.D. were of such importance to Pound that—in one of his final Cantos, "CXIII"—he remembers her saying "serenitas" during the dinner "in pre-history" celebrating the publication of *Des Imagistes* (*Cantos* 801).

Like the relationship between Pound and H.D., each Ezra Pound International Conference has a beginning and ending, but, also like that relationship, each conference provides its attendees with memories, which are now—also like the relationship between H.D. and Pound—intermixed with memories of Pennsylvania and its landscape. Each conference includes excursions that help attendees understand the context of Pound's work. For the Philadelphia conference, attendees were treated to tours of the University of Pennsylvania campus and its surrounding areas, which included a reading of H.D.'s story regarding the young Pound, as a first-year student, wearing colorful socks in defiance of the upperclassmen's established rules of conduct and, as a result, being thrown into a lily pond just behind his dorm room and, for a period, being known as "'Lily' Pound" (*End* 14). A conference tour also went to the Rosenbach Museum and Library, which included a re-creation of Marianne Moore's living room and bedroom, and The Kislak Center itself featured collections of rare books and manuscripts related to Pound, H.D., and William Carlos Williams. Conference attendees were further treated to a tour of the Philadelphia Museum of Art and a trip to Pound's childhood home and to the church his family attended in Wyncote. The post-conference excursion then visited Bryn Mawr College, the school attended by both H.D. and Moore, and East Rutherford and Patterson, New Jersey, to see Williams's homes and the Patterson Falls. Events such as these are always a special part of the conference in that the lives of the poets come off the page and the attendees come to spend time together in a communal atmosphere rarely experienced in academic settings.

We have, thus, collected in this volume works by the poets who read at the conference and pictures that—like the poems, letters, and recollections exchanged between Pound and H.D.—we hope will keep that event and its subjects alive, present, and immediate for our readers. Like the young Pound, then, we ask that "Saint Hilda" pray for us (End 83), and, like the older H.D., we acknowledge the passing of time but cherish *"the first kiss and the last kiss and between, / the surging armies, / [. . .] the shifting scene"* (104).

Works Cited

Doolittle, Hilda. *End to Torment: A Memoir of Ezra Pound*. New York: New Directions, 1979.
——. *Collected Poems, 1912–1944*. New York: New Directions, 1983.
Korg, Jacob. *Winter Love: Ezra Pound and H.D.* Madison: University of Wisconsin Press, 2003.
Pound, Ezra. "A Few Don'ts by an Imagiste." *Poetry* I.6 (March 1913): 200–201.
——. *The Cantos of Ezra Pound*. New York: New Directions, 1989.
——. "Vortex. Pound." *Blast* 1 (June1914): 153–54.
——. "Vorticism." *Early Writings: Poems and Prose*. Ed. Ira B. Nadel. 278–291. New York: Penguin Books, 2005.
Wilhelm, J. J. *Ezra Pound in London and Paris: 1908–1925*. University Park: Pennsylvania State University Press, 1990.

CHARLES BERNSTEIN
Swan Songs

For Richard Sieburth at 70

What you heard is not what I said.
COMMENTARY: You are lying.
COMMENTARY: "What is said" is never absolute.
COMMENTARY: *Meaning is always contextual.*

As the crow flies, so flies the Jew.
COMMENTARY: The Jew exists both in everyday life and in the imaginary.
COMMENTARY: Diaspora is never a whole story.
COMMENTARY: *Low overhead is ideal.*

"Lies are truths that have hardened." (Alan Davies)
COMMENTARY: On the contrary—Truth is lies that have hardened.
COMMENTARY: The problem is not lies but liars.
COMMENTARY: *Truth is difficult.*

"We are rats who build the labyrinth from which we plan to escape."
(Raymond Queneau on OuLiPo practice)
COMMENTARY: On the contrary—We are rats who build labyrinths from which we cannot escape.
COMMENTARY: On the contrary—We are labyrinths who build man. (Even labyrinths have fathers.)
COMMENTARY: *Animalady is a condition not a worldview.*

Stop putting mouths in my words.
COMMENTARY: Resistance precedes presence.
COMMENTARY: Poetry is not speech but speech sounds.
COMMENTARY: *Words are not just what is spoken.*

Written for *Festschrift for Richard Sieburth On the Occasion of His Seventieth Birthday*, ed. Sage Anderson, Paul Fleming, John Hamilton, Daniel Hoffman-Schwar (privately printed for presentation in January 2019).

Phatic not vatic. (Runa Bandyopadhyay)
COMMENTARY: Echopoetics.
COMMENTARY: Identities not identity.
COMMENTARY: [Intentionally left blank]

Knowing what I know today, that much less than before.
COMMENTARY: How much beyond all is whatever is and is today.
COMMENTARY: Even as now is not now and then was not then, still time moves forward, but once and again stops for passengers.
COMMENTARY: *To know nothing is the only positive form of knowledge.*

Metonymy is destiny.
COMMENTARY: Did I tell you to sing?
COMMENTARY: The sun is greater than its sparks.
COMMENTARY: *Even the echoes have echoes.*

The enemy of my enmity is my calamity.
COMMENTARY: Don't say "I told you so" until you're wrong.
COMMENTARY: Indignation intensifies heartburn but is preferable to heart failure.
COMMENTARY: *The enemy of my enmity is my sentimentality.*

The only thing harder than being a poet is being married to one.
COMMENTARY: A reworking of Reb Gimlet's "The only thing harder than being a fool is being married to one," itself a reworking of Reb Negroni's "The only thing harder than being a Jew is being married to one," itself a reworking of Reb Gibson's "The only thing harder than being God is being married to God."
COMMENTARY: Married in the sense of any long-standing intimate relationship.
COMMENTARY: "Poet" here signifies verbal hurdles/hurtles to enlightenment.

Quantum mechanics commands our respect. But an inner voice tells me that this is not yet the real McCoy. The theory provides a lot, but it hardly brings us nearer the old mystery. Anyway, I'm convinced, that it's not a throw of the dice. ["Die Quantenmechanik ist sehr achtung-gebietend. Aber eine innere Stimme sagt mir, daß das doch nicht der wahre Jakob ist. Die Theorie liefert viel, aber dem Geheimnis des Alten bringt sie uns kaum näher. Jedenfalls bin ich überzeugt, daß der nicht würfelt."] (Albert Einstein)
COMMENTARY: But it could be pinochle.
COMMENTARY: Science will never abolish poetry.
COMMENTARY: "Nah ist / Und schwer zu fassen der Gott" (Hölderlin).

Wish, desire, need denied; love hides.
COMMENTARY: An arrow to the heart kills you as dead as a stab in the back.
COMMENTARY: Inside the folds of language are the folds of things.
COMMENTARY: *The hidden pierces the visible at the circumference of the conscious.*

I cannot forgive what I blame you for but which you haven't done.
COMMENTARY: Worse than anything we do is what we fail to do, not by effort but by inattention.
COMMENTARY: Consciousness is culpability.
COMMENTARY: *Irresponsibility is the inability to respond.*

Forget Being, it never liked you anyway.
COMMENTARY: The sign on the screen says, "Accessed Denied."
COMMENTARY: For Marjorie Perloff: Being is a club that beats you to the ground at closing time then opens the next day as if nothing had happened.
COMMENTARY: For Felix Bernstein: Being stumbles, time evaporates, only the traces of trances persist. (Dasein stolpert, zeit ist verflogen, nur die Spuren der Trance bleiben bestehen.)

For love has such a spirit that if it is portrayed it dies. ["ch'Amor mi dona—un spirito in suo stato / che, figurato, —more"] (Cavalcanti)
COMMENTARY: That Love gives me—a spirit in such state / that, figured, —dies.
COMMENTARY: "From Love is won a spirit, in some wise, / Which dies perpetually" (Rossetti).
COMMENTARY: "For Love me gives a spirit on his part / Who dieth if portrayed" (Pound).

Great wisdom's clumsy, true eloquence stutters. [大巧若拙，大辯若訥] (*Tao Te Ching* 45)
COMMENTARY: For Yi Feng: Wisdom is awkward and unruly, eloquence stammers and stumbles.
COMMENTARY: For Ariel Resnikoff: There is nothing more bent than the straight.
COMMENTARY: After Adorno: *the appearance of authenticity is a fabrication.*

Translation is the mother of invention and the father of misunderstanding.
COMMENTARY: Better to stand under, nearer, than to touch. Better still: in between. (Besser unter, näher, als zum Anfassen. Besser noch: Zwischendurch.)
COMMENTARY: You know the story of Russian history, centuries of mayhem and suffering. . . . Then the bad times begin. (Philip Nikolayev)
COMMENTARY: *The authenticity of fabrication is appearance.* (Die Authentizität der Herstellung ist das Aussehen.)

Translation has both an asymptotic desire for closeness verging on fusion and an opposite impulse to distance, to retreat from the otherness of its utterance. These impulses are antipodal and irreconcilable yet reciprocal and, for Hölderlin, ultimately and precariously the same. (Gestützt auf Richard Sieburth)

COMMENTARY: "let no one / Reproach the beauty / Of my homegrown speech / As I go to the fields / Alone, where the lily / Grows wild, without fear." (Sieburth) "Und nicht soll einer / Der Rede Schonheit mir / Die heimadiche, vorwerfen, / Dieweil ich allein / Zum Felde gehe, wo wild / Die Lilie wachst, furchdos" (Hölderlin).

COMMENTARY: "But we shall not look forward / Or back. Let ourselves rock, as / On a boat, lapped by waves" (Sieburth). "Vorwarts aber und riikwarts wollen wir / Nicht sehn. Uns wiegen lassen, wie / Auf schwankem Kahne der See" (Hölderlin).

COMMENTARY: "veiled in song" (Sieburth). "ins Lied / Gehüllt" (Hölderlin).

ELOISA BRESSAN

A Girl

I watered a weed today:
Leaves tickled my ear
And baby sprouts bloomed
into my chest.

My core
—Clutched
in branches—
My head
—carved marble squeezed
by the spleen-reaching
shoots.

I watered my soul's weed
with dropping pearls,
And when I vomited colorful petals
All they saw was a flower.

Steps

You pace in the room—
My heart paces fast—
Your steps mark the doom
Of my flowers' collapse.

From the window I peep
at the joyous dismay
of the people who steep
in the lime I forsake.

On this side of the screen
My narcissus is dead,
I tell you while you preen
In your sculptural step:

My mind is banal—
I think of daffodil symbols—
You don't cross the canal, you
nod your head to the jingle.

I am afraid of the surface
And the depth it conceals,
You walk away from the furnace
That my writing reveals.

Your distraction ignores
the death of my flowers:
My words forge the doors,
Your steps build the towers.

ANDREI BRONNIKOV

Zen Elegies

1.

A gray sky. Waves pound the cliff. A lonely bird is up there.
    What else do you need to be happy?
Between two languages, like Tiresias, with no words and almost
    no feelings,
You weigh your loneliness on scales of the emaciated heart.
Look, you aren't the first one or the last one who is into it,
But you do believe that you are the one who can tell us about it.
Speak, if you can, if the noise of the wind is not driving you crazy.
Speak, if the mad cry of a seagull won't tell us much more.
Speak, if your heart or anything else inside you would not let
    you down—
Since how much is left for you the Sirens on the rocks do not know,
Neither the god from the ancient books nor this grass;
Nobody does. Nature isn't inclined to think or to know.
She simply stands there as a painting on an easel
While someone's observing the landscape, you, me, all our rush,
Observing all this with a mindless look of a baby
By the sea that is washing away our castles of sand
So definitely and forever.

2.

Forget all your misery; after all, you come here to experience at
    least something.
There was nothing like this where you came from; there was no joy
    and no pain.
Only here where your consciousness is becoming alive inside your
    blood in the depths of your veins—
Only here you can see everything as it *is*.
All new cities are similar to the ones that you've seen before;

There is the same twinkle in the eyes of your lover and you
 recognize it,
Though you don't remember where you've seen all this.
You just say: this is mine, and that is not mine.
Your soul is squeezed between heavy stones like a sarcophagus in
 the Egyptian temple.
Your soul senses the gravity of the world—all these countless atoms,
All these mysterious fields and influences—all are pushing on you
 and leaving their traces.
By accumulating all the imprints, step by step, you become
 a replica of this world.
Now, anywhere you go, all will see with whom and where you have
 been, and who you've become.
When you arrived, your soul was like a parchment scroll with
 ancient scripts—
A fragile and thin scroll with mysterious signs and images of
 magical beasts.
When you will have to depart, all this will turn into a landscape;
 wrinkles and voids will appear.
Mountain passes, rivers, woods, cities, islands—everything that
 you have seen will come true.
Everything will materialize; everything will be raised from the
 letters and signs.
Hieroglyphs will turn into roads and their intersections, birds will
 turn into lovers.
Everything will come to life and find its meaning.
The brittle scroll will become elastic, flexible, damp.
Plants and animals will run in the valleys and, higher, in the
 mountains; there will be people there as well.
Only you won't be there.
You'll disappear forever, having given your blood and your flesh
 to the world.
All that was said in those scripts would come true and
 be incarnated,
But you would not see it.

3.

Hurry up, hurry up, as this thin shell is still holding what soon will
    break free.
Hurry up, hurry up, as you still do not know that all your myths
    are just myths.
You have time between this and that, and you have to make choices.
Possession and possibility are behind you; losses and a new search
    lie ahead.
Here—between the Scylla and Charybdis of your feelings—your heart
    is beating like a fish in the hands of brothers from Galilee.
And yet there is hope—this wormwood-like bitterness of life.
Only here, at the threshold of pain, only here anything still can happen.
And this is unstoppable. This is written in the books where
    everything has been accounted for until the very last second.
Where's your place? What do you have to do in order to save just
    a single moment?
You who turn water into wine, can you control a simple timetable?
Can you alter the entire course of the universe to turn it onto your
    own orbits?
Everything has been predicted by the ancients;
Everything, including the departure and arrival times, including
    time to check in and receive the luggage.
Where is a place for at least one of your dark and deep feelings?
They are flying above, not touching anything here.
They are the reflections. But there is no reality either—
    they are the reflections of other reflections.
While you were waiting for her, the earth had moved one million
    miles away.
Now we are in a different place.
The earth is against us—it was always dusty and hard.
The stars are against us—each shot of them hit straight into your heart.
The stars are revived myths. Look, there are so many of them in this
    book!
But you are alone and you don't know where the exit is.
You who speak to the gods, you don't know how to talk to her.

You have no words left; all your words have been used like
    disposable dishes.
You'd better keep silently going on your own way out there—
Above empty lands, above black dazzling skies, in the heights.

4.

Like that ancient king who returned to his island,
All day long you hope for a miracle,
As if there were no places where you could be as you used to be.
Alien cities are in your eyes and a foreign language is
    heard everywhere.
Who are these people who have possessed your heart?
Who are these gods who have driven you into this situation?
No reply. Nature does not know a means to ease your pain.
But you can do it yourself.
See, all is not that bad.
At least, you can make choices now.
You can move, not knowing where you will arrive—
For all that you see is not a guarantee that it is what it is;
And all that you know is too small to be loved,
But it does something to you
And after some time you won't recognize yourself.
Kill the pity for yourself and the others—
Here is the sword with which you cut off the pain.
Kill everything that is not needed for death.
Be prepared for it because it is coming.
It will take you to where you have never been,
You can't drag with you there your mind, love, feelings, money,
Except maybe some coins to pay for the ferry,
Though they'll probably allow someone like you for free.
You'd better stay with us for a while—
Look and see that you don't need tears.
Everything is so unreliable here. One poor instant
    which is lighted up in the dark by an invisible someone.
One moment of loneliness on the seashore

While a ship is sailing away from you, getting smaller and smaller,
Leaving you here all alone with your sorrow.

5.

All the doors are open for you at the top of the day.
The sun shines in dry grasses and burns the ground.
You have been here many times, but haven't seen anything.
Your world was filled with gray clouds of old resentments and illusions.
You always found fault, looking for anyone or anything to blame
    for your failures.
In such a state, you couldn't become a part of nature
Because she doesn't know resentments, and kills and loves with ease.
Isn't it the indifference you were searching for? It was hard to achieve.
Your heart became a stone of tears when your pain came back to you.
That was hard, and you thought: "I can't bear all this anymore."
Imagine if mountains could feel the weight of all their stones—
Then so much screaming and pain would surround us. But this does
    not happen.
Someone has deprived nature of feelings, having left behind
    the sun in the grass,
The bumblebees that are swarming here and there,
The little ants on the rocks.
And then, even smaller, some dust, smaller and smaller—
Something else out there, but still
    the same happy indifference
Of the incredibly small ones.

Excerpts from *Zen Elegies* (Reflections, 2010).

DAVID CAPPELLA

Urge/Surge

one day, the trees   the urge that powers them
infused in me   a sudden, calm strength
to stay still,   immersed in silence

surge upward   the slow rise toward light
their sky-push   no matter what
like a slow current   winding its way through me

their rooted surge   deep in the soil
bores hard,   drilling straight through
faintest fears   planting firm grips of hope

there   gazing at their canopy
rooted where   to their root tips under ground
grope   nourishing ground.

Nafplion Afternoon

The cicadas—
loud, scratching
in the palm trees.
Their chorus, the ancient
Mediterranean singing
deep into the heavy air.
The heat—an eddying swirl:
the hazy agate sky—Athena's eye.

Closing Time at the Ontological Hotel

You must do something:
so you order in.
Night falls too fast.

Time, like a stubborn cough,
will not go away. It's there
for you in slivers of neon green.

The curtains—drawn.
The bed—turned down,
dainty chocolates on two pillows.

Life sits there on the side
of the bed. It wants to nestle
with you. You gaze at the radio.

You imagine time: a great white horse,
nostrils flaring, wild-eyed, charging
to send you reeling back on your heels.

You sit in the corner chair,
untying your shoes. A fear jolts
you, an emotional TIA

scalds your perception,
a little sting that burns
your nerves.

Still, life sulks, waiting—
the bedside lamplight
cuts a razor slice across

the tightly made bed.
Because the universe
is expanding

you know it's time
to brush your teeth
to feel your gums.

You imagine time pulling
a chariot, sweeping down
out of the mirror.

The Horae urge the steed,
hell bent, you can tell.
its eyes are aflame.

You think: I'll be trampled.
But then dinner arrives…
that's how your life is.

MARY DE RACHEWILTZ

Poet on the BBC

The Poet suffered agonies
in flesh and blood, all inward
a placid bosom for an altar
he missed when young.
    Pneumatic bliss
found late in a lifetime spent
on knees & lighting candles.

The wife displayed with her jewelry
the riches made by selling cats.
She had the Poet's name engraved
on public Banks and Libraries.
The bourgeois hand
    learnt how to dress;
a rising instinct did the rest.

For Katha

Something within her there is
doesn't like walls and barriers
spiked & ridged with cutting shards.

Something in her is governed
by wood's clear demarcation,
for fences make good neighbors.

Through lattice the eyes can see
the voice converse and carry
news of laughter and sorrow.

2006

For Eva

I

Lady Eve despised the apple:
        she ate the serpent
and donned the shed skin,
never bought the leopard
in the show-window, wore
raw silk and cashmere instead.
She alone has improved
        the Poet's line, sent
Dallmayr marzipan and French
chocolate, not a Boston marriage,
offered the old man
        her mother's best bed.

Oh you scholars, pay homage,
stop bickering & sing, *Gloria!*

II

Both Eva and I agreed
there is but little talent
but some honesty in me.
So let me ask her many
nice and curious visitors
why doesn't he, whoever
reaps the fruit of her labors,
bring the many translations
and the books she has written
and line them up on the shelf?
Surely, all the Poets would step
out of the air to rumba,
foxtrot and waltz, and tango
with a girl in a bikini
into heaven's ever blue.

If I now say my grandson
was put on a butcher's block
in Kindergarten, they'll think
I am mad when the moon grows
and I cut my hair because
my nurse told me to and my
mother feared I'll marry one
writing poetry.
                Beware
of the greedy gray tabby
debating as to what would
the wise old friend Possum say.

Mesmerism

I

Reading Browning—how
   Pound not merely read
but physically
   experienced the thing
the older poet felt
   and saw open eyed.
Young and mesmerized
   he prayed in fear of
the price extolled by
   Beauty as seen
when under the spell
   of a greater soul
who recognized Truth
   in bright blinding light.

II

When the Schloss was pronounced *shlosh*
and it turned out
   the Prince *war kein Prinz*
Sister Bernetta said:
   "to the manner born."
With allure and spunk
of a true blue blood colt
the little princess danced
fear and shame
into the blue.

Years gone by, he came
   on a cold Christmas day
bearing a gilt and leather-bound book,
   the family heirloom.

Like his mother, the child wanted
        pretty things,
a beautiful object, confusing
        language and religion
in an immature mind.

An Old Proverb

An old proverb says: Ideas
are colored by what they are dipped in—
that wine is milk for the aged
when the search for a family tree
supplants the daily cross-word.

I would fain quote Liz Browning
who claimed "books are the better men,"
then add of my own: that memory
is the best garden to cultivate
and belief is in what you have seen.

Should aging eyesight fail you,
stand by the tree of Good & Evil
grown strong in well-tilled ground with many
apples, with multicoloured carnations,
with birds singing merrily.

If in a dark night the owl
and the ravens flutter and craw-craw,
follow the blind who said: I can pray,
God will solve the puzzle, let the young
move on with the speed of light.

January 17, 2009

PATRIZIA DE RACHEWILTZ

The Blue-Stoned Bracelet

Under the cherry-tree boughs
leaves whispering
pre-antic dawns,

your deep dark eyes glowing still
with stars, falling, falling,

into a hollow wishing well....

A sudden light-ray fell
on your blue-stoned bracelet,

twice entwined,

as two lovers yearn
but can not meet

& thus hold love
more precious

than ocean-wide absences
of topaz-jewelled waves,

unbreakable,

yet free....

Did You Get My Little Sun?

In sleep
ride the waves
that carry you beyond
the shallow banks
over the sharp dented riff
into the open sea shell
gently, gently, closing
and making you
its own precious pearl

that is what you are for me

In My Days and Nights

I wrote ballads in my head
            until the moon was almost
                                    full

I picked rosemary
  & lilac flowers
     in the still quiet afternoon

I heard a whooshing
           terrifying sound
  a man sailing in the sky
      crashed into the rocks
                    below

I found the crown of yellow petals
   dumped on the heap
      of leaves & trash

     this made me sad

I hung it on the garden wall
         to remember I still care

while you walked
        in the city of poets
              & canals

A cello played
        & my heart wept
              with joy & hope

The moon still almost full
      will have a smile
            tomorrow

the citronella candle
      reflected in your eyes

           …

White Sails

Moon bells high & bronze heavy
  up in the cathedral tower
ring in the chained ghosts to me
  into the far away.
Red autumn butterfly wings
  fly my withered songs
  back to the wind swollen sails
  with the sweet mirth
of the captain's poet's eyes
who, in undilutable ink,
   wrote the magic words
    "Stay … this is paradise"

Untitled

Good night
  sweet
    butterfly
      of the night
a star shines
  always
    for you

The Green Grotto

She holds a handful of
                miniature plums
yellowed by the early fall's sun
in the green grotto—
the shadow of the mountain
                looming high—
an absence lingers
                by the grey walls,
a poet' s wish on the gnarled branch
falls gently on her
                luminous face
as slowly she walks on
with the taste of plums
                and summer's ending.

SILVIA FALSAPERLA

Beach Scene

At the seaside in Versilia you and I
Sat on the sand with the seashells we collected,
Bugles and fans and blue-black mussels,
Sea potatoes and seaweed washed ashore.
These were our props, our beach toys.
The creative sea was our garden.
We dug up the sand with our hands or
Used sticks, the bark peeling, smooth as bone.
We built the Great Wall of China,
Highways and roads all covered with shells
And dug deep deep holes that touched the sea beneath us.
We played silently as two children,
The sparks of sun on the sea
That watched us and gurgled with the sound of the waves—
And then you interrupted us,
The man with the wallet in his pocket
That pulses like a tongue
And beats a tune that goes like this:
If it isn't bought, it isn't real.
And despite our protests,
You announced that you would get us
A pail and shovel from one of the miscellany shops along the road.

After an hour you came back with a big plastic shopping bag
And a cigar between your fingers.
You spilled the beach toys on the sand, a red pail with blue and white stripes,
A red shovel, a red rake, obscene and blaring, aliens or burlesque women.
They disturbed our play and we became erratic.
We demolished the Great Wall, the highway with the red rake and the red shovel,

A cataclysm in the defeated evening.
The sea ignored them, reclaiming the shells and the sticks
The sea ignored and erased the human footprint with five toes
Levelling it with the sand as the flaps of the waves spilled over.

The Piano

A neighbour threw out an old piano
on the driveway next to the sidewalk,
an unusual throwaway.

I have seen them all:
mattresses, swivel chairs, coffee tables, old hockey sticks,
hundreds of items discarded
waiting for rescue or the garbageman.

People stop to look at the piano,
but it's too damn heavy to carry away.

Out for a stroll in the afternoon
I press my finger on a key,
a musical note springs out, a celestial sound.
The old piano works.

When I return, a girl with a screwdriver tries
to dismantle the piano
so that she can carry it away,
but then thought better of it.

At dusk when the tv hypnotizes and we are all lonely strangers,
piano music streams in with the balmy air
from open windows and balconies.
We become a tribe again.

The next day the piano is still there.
A man gets off his bike and rolls his fingers on the keys, singing a jazzy
    soulful tune.
Later the screwdriver-girl returns and people cluster around her play-
    ing and singing.
None of the neighbours complaining, the driveway becomes a village.

As I roll into the driveway on my bike, I hear two men conspire
to take the bronze pieces from the piano.

Two days later when I thought the piano was to stay
I saw it collapsed on the driveway,
a fallen prize animal, the keys were teeth scattered, intestines strewn,
offended and disemboweled
for its bronze parts,
a carcass now.

Leonardo Kaneshige

The brazilian sun crossed by two strains,
italic face, nipponic eyes
an utterance, a laugh
I've heard before in memory, a rush to origins,
a promenade with you in an elegant boulevard
of a baroque mediterranean city.

The grace of a still wind,
your eyes swim in southern seas
and melt in the sparkle of my white sweater.

Your name is Art.
I am your sakura.
I am your mona lisa.

Your body is Art
sculptured by the florentine father of
David.

J. RHETT FORMAN

Uncle Sam, the Repo Man

Then there was Sam Jr.
who should've had the house
except for it was unfinished
and so it passed to Joe Abby
because Sam preferred to work
and Abby did not

and when he and Abby
after a long trip and a short war
arrived back in Dallas
on the train from Fort Travis
after the wet trench and the march
the steamer and the parade in New York
the oldest hitched it east and Sam west
to Oak Cliff where he became
a messenger of fate
and an executor of justice
in all a repossession man

But, Uncle Sam, she's lyin' in it!
Grab hold, boy!

in nineteen fifty-two
two years more a boy
John Reuben awoke before dawn
and caught the Wallace boy goin' west
to Henderson from Pine Hill
and from there hitched it
with a telephone man
as far west as Mesquite
and waited all afternoon

under the mesquite trees
no one driving by in the heat
until some goat-roper
who spoke little and smoked much
let him in the truck bed
with the hay and a Mexican
tan like a wet haystack
and dropped him off on Houston Street
and in those days a streetcar ran
Deep Ellum to Oak Cliff
clear west of the Trinity

Whose boy are you?
Abby's.
Abby's boy's grown and you ain't.
That's Maurice.
Well, nephew, you work?
Two hands, two feet.
Katy, go an' git the cot. We'll setcha in the kitchen.

and that summer they went out
in the day to the whites
at night to the blacks
as far west as Grand Prairie
and in the morning
they'd pick up Tommy
that is Freedman
whose grandfather lit out west
to flee his bonds and the bondsman
to clean cattle pins in Fort Worth
twenty years until the gout hit him
Tommy paid same as Johnny
spent a fourth on five cent
John Ruskin cigars
and a fourth on whiskey

a fourth on gamblin'
and a fourth on Missy Jade
Jade like her jade-green eyes
jadestone set in obsidian

Woman, I will take this bed with you in it!
She too fat, Sam!

We went out one night,
Uncle Sam, Tommy, and myself
to west Dallas where the blacks lived,
and Sam meant to get the bed
this family defaulted on.
I do not mean to say
he wanted to take it—
just that that was his job,
a repo man, a repossession man,
at that particular time.
And so we meant to get this bed
from this woman:

Grab hold, Johnny!

and Tommy and Johnny and Sam
heaved the bedframe
out from under the woman

And she hits the floor so hard
she breaks through the floorboards,
so Tommy and me haul the bed out,
chuck it into the truck bed
while Sam's in there pullin' this woman—
whose bed we just took—outta the floor.

and Tommy and Johnny tied it down
and as soon as Sam got her out of the floor
she took a pan to Sam's head

And as Sam's running out,
we hear a baby crying from the back room.
So he turns around, takes a pan to the face,
and throws her back down into the floor:

Git yourself up and back at it.
That baby in there needs feedin'.

and Tommy and John Reuben starred
and both thought there was
some mercy in that act
even if the woman had no bed to sleep in
and no man to sleep in it with

Sam got in the truck and they drove
across the Trinity west to Oak Cliff
and Sam a man of few words
and most of them coarse
drove silent through the streetlights

and in the night through Oak Cliff
the cicadas sang from the Trinity
and Tommy's face glowed
like the ember of a John Ruskin cigar
black in the smoke-light

The Americaniad

I found Zeus' grave in the cemetery
down in the holler

sometimes on Sunday afternoons
Aunt Polly would read from a great big book about Zeus
it told how Pastor Zeus got to be a fine preacher
at the Assembly of God in Mount Olympus
which Granddaddy said was across the river
in Indiana north of Evansville

that was back in the Civil War when some Yankee
stole the bride off this Indian chief

and all the other chiefs and all the Yankees went at it
until eventually Cochise came back from his ships
and slaughtered a whole mess of Yankees
like fatted calves and even whipped the river

and Cochise dragged that Yankee boy's corpse
behind his horse until the President made him give it back

I asked Granddaddy if the President put Cochise
out in Oklahoma with the Creeks and the Cherokees
and the Comanches and the rest of them

he said no Cochise died a free man in Arizona
I admit I was pretty happy he did

Gold Rush

Skeeter slept in a bear hide
I think even the cabin has rickets
they're on the road to Alaska I suppose
wouldn't it be something all that gold

I bet it smell sweet blood
I bet it run hot honey
I bet it do

if the tax man come or the census taker
tell him I'm through shoot 'em hell I don't care

Skeeterbug, Skeeterbug, we're home
when she woke up in the back seat
and saw the Milky Way
for years she thought they'd driven from Dallas
to some strange and distant star

sometimes I dream the Milky Way is a horseshoe
and the sky a spotted pinto
and the moon its rider raiding north

sometimes the night bleeds molten ore
sometime it drip hot honey
sometime it do

JOHN GERY

Descant on Pennsylvania

Pennsylvania has never had an earthquake
in my lifetime, nor massive starvation,
nor a plague to kill more than the legionnaires—
nor has its west fallen victim to forest fires
yet, nor its southeast to secession by farmers,
nor its northeast to anarchic coalminers (despite
several half-hearted attempts), nor has any leader
been skinned for his corruption, or shot, hanged,
and strung up by his heels with his mistress,
nor has it had a revolution against itself (unless
you count the Hessians as part of itself), while
those who disappeared at Gettysburg in a day
still remain among us as celebrated ghosts, nor
have dinosaurs sprung to life here, as in Arizona
and New Mexico, nor have meteors descended on
the plain folk, nor have the poets who once lived here
—Stevens, H.D., Jeffers, Pound—returned, although,
while he shunned serious verse himself, Ben Franklin
did transform Philadelphia into his exotic workshop.

Nor has the music made here gained much fame
worldwide, let alone in state, though its music played
eventually goes everywhere, nor have the women
born here, after drinking the water as young girls
and eating eggs fresh each morning, risen to be
among the world's great beauties, nor does industry (steel,
auto parts, concrete blocks, coffins, scissors, bedspreads,
whether of those who work or those who tell workers
how to do their jobs) bow in awe of Pennsylvania's
power to mesmerize and disarm, nor do fish leap wildly
into the fisherman's net, nor do domestic dogs,

in spite of their avidly wagging tails, perform tricks
their owners can barely imagine. Few dine in the nude,
the Altoona flood has receded, Hershey's boys have grown
into men he himself could never become, and no one,
so far as I know, orchestrated Three Mile Island. No,
Pennsylvania is hardly worth the price of the paper
of the maps we've printed to find our way home.

But things sublime belong, thought Aristotle,
in the middle distance. Or as M. Moore of Carlisle
might put it: "In your very cunningly / Wrought /
Modesty, / You are the Naught / And the everything."*

---

* "Wisdom at Last" (previously unpublished poem), in *The Poems of Marianne Moore* (Ed. Grace Schulman, New York: Viking, 2003), 33.

Suburban Prejudice

O give me a home
on the outskirts of Rome
or a maison d'ville
perched atop Chestnut Hill

where the thrashers lay eggs
irregardless of snags
that twist ankle or foot—
a roost safe for my root!

>   *Refrain:*
>   *Safe, safe on the edge*
>   *where my property's lined with a hedge*
>   *where seldom is raised an objection well-phrased*
>   *nor rebuke to whate'er I allege.*

May my secrets keep hid
like preserves under lid
where sundials keep time
undeterred by the grime

that festers in downspouts
or shrivels my bean sprouts
spreading slowly next door
to creep up through the floor.

>   *Refrain*

May my shed house no rats,
my front lawn no crab grass,
may my gables yield roses
granting shelter to toadses.

When my shutters fly open,
may my glass stay unbroken
and the light enter through to
the sights I've grown used to,

   Refrain

but if I should close them,
let no other suppose them
other than darkened space,
shielding safely my face,

nor, should I rip out my porch,
set my kitchen to torch,
or demolish my cursed house,
think me daft as a church mouse.

   Refrain

Build a wall to wall squirrels out,
neighborhood boys and girls out,
city folk in for the day,
or the squatters who stay.

If I wangle my shot gun
and fire at them not just one,
but three rounds, let them flee
from my dear privacy!

   Refrain

And when my Lord arrives
to lift me to the skies,
may my parlor be neat,
with no dust on His seat,

and the credo I've sworn to
in this realm I was born to
serve me equally well
in either Heaven or Hell.

   Refrain

Ruffed Grouse

Official State Bird of Pennsylvania

Is this my last chance
or my first, drubbing
against corn stalks, sticks
none broke here, askance
the field's edge, hob in,
small nuts that squirrel picks

by me, disturbing
nothing, too busy
working against this cold,
safe I'll stay, curb in
on this log, lusty
to fret in her fold

she seems alert to,
as she nips that ant
there, slow as this worm
I avoid, turn to
only when I can't
find morsels or charm

from her striped white breast
mites or ticks. What sticks
is her texture, frill
ridged back, thick crest
upwards: Something clicks—
a hawk or joy? Chill

means hurry. I'm old,
without an egg place,
must exploit that red:
Others mourn, or scold,
who scuffs in this race
none has won nor fled.

Decoy

How did I get inside this
body, not another? How
I'd prefer *his*, flamingo-
like, yet not ostentatious,
or that flicking orange glow
behind that blind there. To scowl

or not makes no difference,
this sawdust in me settles
as indigestion awry—
and she draws no inference
I am alive, nor fettles
my spine for herself. To cry

will seem but an act, not me,
a wood corpse, painted feathers,
tied to one spot like the sedge
to the riverbank, or tree
I'll never scale that pleasures
her mate. Drift to the far edge

to register both out there
and in here, someone to mark
the aura around her by, hard
as rock or door stop, to care
and protect, not breathe, no spark
of danger here, my canard

to be the target no one
aims for, I float on the waves
made by others passing by.
O, burn off my colors, sun!
Fade me. Held fast by my staves,
monument to whom can't fly.

JEFF GRIENEISEN

On Our Thirteenth Anniversary

Sample these years,
a baker's dozen, the lace year,
each year a day in the fest of St. Anthony,
answering prayers for what is lost.
Through all that we've lost,
what a story we've created:

Once, an angel ordered me a drink,
                phoned it in
to the bar near her home.
We staggered through snow
        "where is the highway tonight?"
What hippie dream is this?
            The woman I love disappeared
into the hallway,
lying where I found her,
        lying beside her.
No pressure
              to love, no pressure to find my way
around the world.

We share our anniversaries
              with Imagists, Poundians,
no Midwest vacations of silent cabins,
clinking fragile champagne glasses.
            And ain't it the truth—you and me
            against the world.

This note's for you, my love.
I remember each moment like a tat of lace,
webbed by the careful hands of an old woman
        in Burano.

So many firsts in my life:
>	glimpses of flower pot chimneys over London
>	wandering through Père Lachaise graves
>	eating ice cream beneath the Eiffel Tower
>	closing down Hofbräuhaus

In Italian "fare tredici," "to do 13," means
to hit the jackpot.
you might call me "Mr. Jackpots."
In the lottery of my life
I'm blessed to have found you,
my wife, now of the Long Dozen years.

Other 13's:
>   In Valhalla, Loki the trickster
arrived to feast as the uninvited guest.
In old Jerusalem, on Mount Zion,
13 gathered for the last supper of all last suppers.
1300 years later, on Friday the 13th,
Knights of the Templar were assassinated.
Some would tell us to steer clear of 13,
>	skip to 14 and count
>>	ourselves lucky.

But I came into the world on the 13th day,
and every 1/13 means I've survived
another year.

For us, now, 6/19 will be 13 years
from that beginning
in that ballroom, from castle theme
>	to the castle on the Italian mountainside.

And I count myself a simple, lucky husband.

Sketch

She woke
to the near-finished sketch
of herself
sleeping
in the hostel
on top of Montmartre,
the last lines
on her fingers
curled, unseen
under her chin.

She stretched
beneath scratchy sheets
before we all had to leave
for the day. The staff
stripped and made bunks,
wiped down communal showers.

We spent another day in Paris,
another metro ticket,
waiters asking:
Jambon? Oui, Jambon.

Still she sleeps
on thick paper shoved
between brochures of Tower Bridge
and the Vatican,
always between cities
where she lives her summers.

The Ring

I twist this ring
into the pale groove it's left
after only six months.

I'm no more able to live
without it as I am able to sit
without my wallet

pressing into familiar spaces.
I need to feel this band,
to spin it while I think of words

when I'm not sure
what words to use
as if it's a golden decoder.

As a knuckle exists
only where two bones meet,
this ring is just a space between our souls,
a ring because it's missing a center.

Particles of gold flake off
as I grasp iron railings or run
my hand along the ancient stone walls
of our Tirolean honeymoon.

More shavings scrape off
against U.S. East Coast doorknobs
in our new house.

This ring never shrinks,
but bits smaller than dust
lost to the ground, must resurrect,

find a way to band together again
or remain lost forever
among the shifting earth.

THOMAS HEFFERNAN

These poems relate to Pound's practices thematically. In the *Cantos*, Pound referenced actual pivotal historical events, as does my poem regarding 9/11, below. Especially as the *Cantos* began, Pound had in mind Browning's dramatic monologues. Several short monologues are here excerpted from my collection, *Working Voices*. One is about incorporation of original language; several concern uses of money, likewise thematic in Pound's works. Recalling Imagism, I close with haiku.

Soon It Will Be Ten Years:
Lines Written on Sept. 4, 2011

Now and then, during the last hour,
when I have glanced out the window,
the dove has been there, the same spot
on the same telephone wire,
a shade of gray, scarcely moving.
The color and the bird reminds
and doesn't remind of a day
when morning broke, from blue to gray.

The dove on the wire is alone.
Uncommon, and odd: every dove
I've seen before was with a mate.
and something else I'd seen comes back—
a wire stretched between the towers,
the aerialist walking it
back and forth, the marvel of mind
and skill and maybe luck that wind

or misstep hadn't plummeted
him headlong down through breathless air,
another singular being.
He chose to occupy his time

doing what he alone could do.
He took a more visible way
than most, who, also, every one,
have one life, one time, that's their own.

This early September Sunday,
so near to the day of the tenth
year, I pray for those whose bodies,
in desperate courage not to burn
alive, plummeted; pray for all
who died; and hope for those suffering
loss and memory of loss, that they
have faith love did not die that day.

I look out the window. The dove
has gone, has flown. The words *mourning
dove* come to mind, and how, native
where accent sounded them alike,
as a boy I had wondered if
the bird's name wasn't *morning dove*.
Now, both feelings are connecting:
I mourn; I'm glad it is morning.

Adam's Eve

Consider the tale of Adam and Eve,
How innocence ended with Adam's eve,

And not only his eve but Eve's eve, too,
The pair of them wearing coverings that leave

A peculiar feeling when a person
Is used to freedom from pant leg and sleeve....

You may suppose that, awakened from Eden
And timeless bliss, they forgot to perceive

What, earlier on, happy and childlike,
They knew: —but things connect: were they to believe

In that new world, new place; were they able
To wonder, to feel changes that swell, heave,

Hurtle into Time, down highways, byways,
Dead ends and thoroughfares, days and years weave?

Maybe they knew, how not to see, shadows,
When shadows may spoil joys that would relieve?

O writer, might such questions enlighten?
Twining breaths rise and fall eve after Eve.

Translator

Si, signore, so, I will try versions
of the verses: Leopardi, he touches
me very much; our feelings agree, yes.
Si, translation is treason, we Italians
say. *Allora,*
         Just so, to know Shakespeare,
we must learn English, *si,* to feel his mind
and heart. Just so, you feel Dante, his kind
of life, his cosmos, sphere inside sphere,
in his language, best.
         Ma, esempio,
truly I appreciate how some who
work his triple verse try and try and try,
to jump from tongue to tongue, to make beauty.
But...
   è vero? Truth, did Dante ever get,
into English, words I cannot forget?

Banker, Banking

Why shouldn't a banker be Secretary
of the Treasury? Conflict of interest
be damned—makes sense that guys who know money
understand what to do, and they're the best
choice to do interface between Wall Street
and the ninety-eight percent. You complain?
Look, people on minimum wage, they get
twelve, thirteen grand a year, some CEOs gain
twenty-five thousand a day, so what's new?
The return of robber barons, you say?
a Golden Age only golden for a few?
Give yourself a break, don't fight it, the lay
of the land is survival—we know who's
fittest the more we see whose money grows.

A Different Banker

I didn't study banking in college,
not seriously—I used a dummy,
a fake account. I made imaginary
dollars, enough that I could leverage
into real money, meaning that I took
the hint. I took up investing for real,
a difference being I wanted to peel
away poverty from poor people, make

right conditions, writing micro-loans. I
became invested in helping women,
I worked at a Grameen-type bank to loan
small sums for start-up. Chose Indonesia—
took courses in the language, and so learned
about many things, experience I earned.

Billionaire

My only luxury, as I see it,
is the Jacuzzi in the jumbo jet.
The plane itself is a necessity (yet
my wife complains, she says it's a "his," nit-
picking at me, and wants a "hers.") First
time I had a billion, I felt fulfilled
for a while, then made more, then more. Then, would
you believe, I lost balance between best
and good—losing time I can't replace to
build wealth I can get more of, up markets
or down. Recent blood tests showed weird platelets.
And when I feel tired, I know what to do—
keep making money, it's how I feel good.
My business will carry on when I'm dead.

A Different Billionaire

I don't bother with having a huge house,
let alone six or seven. I may be
"worth billions" as the phrase goes, but am I
my money or am I myself?… My grouse?

False beliefs. Like, the rich are job-makers.
The fact: we spend a fraction of our money.
But when middle and poorer people buy,
their money circulates—to grocery stores,

landlords, gas stations, thrift shops, goes the cash
they have to live. When half a country's wealth
is owned by half a hundred people, the health
of the body politic is bound to crash.
The common good or the common worse is
what's ahead, between them is what's to choose.

Pilot

Do you believe a flight will be off course
almost a hundred percent of the time?
The automatic pilot like a mime
(of me) brings it back to true, like the boss
it really is, except for landing and take-off.
Off course so much, but guided, I'm assured
is true, true as fact? As metaphor? Blurred,
I ask myself does it matter what rough
bent of meaning applies, so long as right
aeronautics do? My brother says math
is full of paradox, like the weird truth
that one system has parallel lines to meet
at infinity, what I would say is true
when deep cloud breaks into endless blue.

A Haibun

His name was Lionel by then, 'little lion'. In New England a cat his color is 'orange', in Japan 'cha-iro'; tea-colored. He had become handsome. 'what a beautiful face', people said. Not something commonly said of a cat, but it was
true. His eyes, the irises striated in shades of light and dark gold, matched patterns
of fur on his heart-shaped face.

>   syringe and sick cat
>   on a stainless table...
>   waft of summernight air
>   (*Modern Haiku*, 25, 3)

The original distemper couldn't be cured. Blood transfusions by staff at the Faculty of Agriculture Veterinary Hospital prolonged his life.

He had the strangest tail. It zig-zagged, in reversing hairpin turns, diminishing into a vanishing point at the tip.

***

street ice...
a card in our mailbox
back unopened
            (*Modern Haiku*, 49.2. (2018)

RODOLFO BRANDÃO DE PROENÇA JARUGA

Canto I

E assim descer ao navio,
dar quilha às ondas contra o mar divino e
mastro e vela alçarmos sobre aquela negra nave,
a bordo dela a carregar ovelhas e também os nossos corpos
graves, lacrimantes, e ventos vindos pela popa
a nos inflar a vela e nos levar além,
artifício de Circe, a deusa de belos cabelos.
Embarcados e com o vento a reger o leme,
à vela cheia avançamos sobre o mar até o fim do dia.
Sol a seu repouso, sombras sobre o oceano,
às lindes nós chegamos das mais fundas águas,
territórios de Ciméria, cidades populosas
cobertas por espessa névoa jamais varada
pela luz do sol,
nem quando se estende às estrelas, nem quando desce do céu,
noite a mais negra ali se estende sobre miseráveis.
Na vazante do Oceano, nós atracamos no local
que nos predisse Circe.
Ali Euríloco e Perímedes cumprem os ritos
e eu saco a espada da bainha
e cavo a cova cubital.
Vertemos libações aos mortos,
primeiro hidromel e depois vinho e água salpicada com farinha branca.
E então rezei aos mortos exangues, e rezei muito,
tornado a ítaca estéreis touras das melhores
em sacrifício, a cobrir de dons a pira,
e uma ovelha inteira pra Tirésias, negra ovelha-guia.
Sangue escuro escorre pela fossa,
almas vêm do Érebo, de cadáveres de noivas,
de rapazes e de velhos tão sofridos;
almas maculadas por lágrimas recentes, meninas tenras,

e homens muitos mutilados pelo bronze das lanças,
mortos de guerra que inda portam cruentas armas.
Essa multidão me rodeava. Gritando pálido,
a meus homens clamo por mais bestas,
por gado degolado, ovelhas imoladas pelo bronze.
Vertido unguento, aos deuses clamo,
a Plutão o forte e a louvada Prosérpina.
Desembainhada a espada
afastei da fossa os impetuoso mortos impotentes
até que enfim eu pudesse ouvir Tirésias.
Porém quem vem primeiro é Elpenor,
nosso amigo Elpenor,
insepulto, abandonado a céu aberto,
carcaça deixada na casa de Circe,
sem velório e sem mortalha, já que outras lides nos urgiam.
Apiedado peito. Clamei-lhe sem demora:
"Êlpenor, por que arte você veio a esta costa escura?
Você veio a pé, sobejando marujos?"
  E ele grave:
"Mau fado e vinho farto, no lar de Circe adormeci.
Descendo a larga escada descuidado, caí contra a pilastra,
a nuca estraçalhada, a alma lançou-se ao Averno.
Mas eu lhe imploro, meu senhor, não me abandone
sem velório e sem sepulcro, recolhe as minhas armas,
erige a minha tumba à beira mar, inscrito:
Um homem sem fortuna e com a fama a porvir.
E finca em pé meu remo, o que entre amigos eu ginguei."

E veio Anticleia, a quem contive, e aí Tirésias Tebano,
portando o seu cajado douro, notou-me e por primeiro disse:
"Por segunda vez? Por que, ó desgraçado,
a enfrentar os mortos desolados e esta triste terra?
Afasta-te da fossa, deixa-me beber do sangue
para o vaticínio.
  E eu recuei

e o velho forte pelo sangue então me disse: "Ulisses,
terás retorno por Netuno rancoroso, negros mares,
todos os teus pares perderás. E aí veio Anticleia.
Jaz em paz Divus, eu digo, isto é Andreas Divus,
in officina Wecheli, 1538, vindo de Homero.
E ele navegou entre as sereias, ali e além
e até Circe.
    Venerandam,
no verso do cretense, co'a coroa douro, Afrodite,
cypri munimenta sortita est, sorridente, orichalchi,
com douradas faixas e colares, tu, de pálpebras escuras,
portando o ramo douro do Argicida. E eis que:

JUSTIN KISHBAUGH

Black Water II

With knees crossed on white chair,
he blows with spenders,
sometimes sore lips,
white pants, and a head bob
that marks time
with whines and moans from below
as one with rice grains in a tin can

keeps a measured beat

while another on bike rim
tiptoes a 4/4 across silvery waves
as he on keys
catches a covert chord
and, with head tilt
and wide eyes,

says something in that pregnant moment
about an opening or play about to be made

and fills in with sweet digressions
of hot hotel rooms with overhead fans
or a white-sun beach with misty breeze,

and, beholding,

I lick lips with tongue tip
to tease a direction

with movements, I think, of proper stroke

and, maybe, in step with
she, all cotton and lip gloss,
beaded, holding a tall glass,
and, wiping brow,

       I raise
    hands in praise

as he standing with alto
spreads evening
golden-pink
across this earthen canvas
and seems to admit with one long note:

  "we might be out here
     all night boys
but eventually we'll get home."

Keef Swagger

Metal
    fuzz riffs   punctuate
          like   pistons   constant
from shoulder   tip   and snarled grin
that streams smoke and strikes sin from iron
wrought   by hammer   on anvil
and a track   marked   arm
that plunges   in the repetition of rhythm
                          and abrupt
                          upstroke

  Razor slash   chords rip   from fingertip and tourniquet;
  the engine   on this train is as important   as its course,
  silence   as necessary   as the chord   tarred fuel
  that combusts   in your lungs   and veins

      An outsider at twenty,
      an exile at twenty eight

  Armed   with axe,   needle,   and Anita
  you   found   left of   center
  lacking   light so   you   wrapped
  yourself   in   shadows   and filled
                the darkness with   a spectral gleam
                          skull ring and Moroccan scarf

    A skeleton father   who slithers swagger and
    sidles sideways   handcuffed at the wrist and
    self-consciously   marked for death

A flame   more tame now within   your lungs and veins
glimmers   within   your eyes,   smile,   and face,
but if   you   tempt   the devil   with silver
he will   linger   within   that skin   and
hide behind   those eyes and wait   and wait   forever
    with another cigarette   ready to burn

Serious Moonlight

Afternoon seemed a myriad of armadillos and astronomers.
I wore scrubs for some reason, and wool socks kept my feet
warm in duck-boots. Cattails rose to 7ft, and mist held close
to the pond's surface.   Initially,
it seemed out of   Green-hill   the way, but
standing there   red   with the sun
all orange, resting   *hair*   above the mountains,
it did seem like   *a r m s*   a postcard or Renoir
painting.   basket   dress   Thus, being certain of
my affection,   *le gs* and candles   the possibilities
of evening   seemed inevitable.
Each movement took on weight as if previously filmed and
we merely inhabited a playback. I like my life as a
movie; it's easier to continue to the next scene.
Her voice, somehow feline, defined itself with
padded steps, and, post projecting pebbles pondward,
the appropriate decision was to progress in our time-shared.
                    The radio played Bowie, the wine
Green-glass   cork was removed, and the candles
    wine   were lit. Tuna fish didn't interest me,
    laughs echo   but I ate half a sandwich. Wine droplets
    hash's   spilled on your leg, and I questioned
    carnival   whether it was a lack of tolerance,
                    nervousness, or clumsiness.
The intrigue passed and I offered combustible desserts.
Night became a flat rock, candles, and moonlight, as stories were
exchanged over   bottles of wine. Surprisingly,
insects were not   moonlit   a factor in
our location, thereby   silken   allowing you
my full attention.   songs   I became fascinated
with your mannerisms,   throb   and watched your tongue
run across your bottom lip. like drowning Silent moments of
positioning occurred, but   the sharing of
          breath compelled us forward.

MARY MAXWELL

Exercise

Even though she taught them herself, my mother forbade me from classes in creative writing. And when, in due course, the time came to disobey her, she took my betrayal with as much grace as any orthodoxy might when one of its own strays far from the fold's proscriptions. One exercise she had her students perform sent them out into the long corridor outside her office; their assignment was to describe the curious configuration of cracks on the purposeless end wall some clumsy renovations had created. For students with aptitude the experience was, without exception, she contended, a "breakthrough," and at semester's end they would ask of her the hour's secrets. She smiled sagely but revealed nothing. The shameful truth, as she told it to me, was that the exercise had come about one day she herself had needed solitude to attempt, once again, to finish her own work. Nevertheless, she insisted, the exercise itself was not a sham, for it forced her students to acknowledge then overcome the limits of their resources, that self-imposed ordeal any real poet will have to undergo herself. *What long ago suggested the periplum has become since your death this perplexing web. I try to navigate its tangled confusion of lines – my lines, your lines, Pound's viscous filaments. I set out once again to claim that troubled legacy only to be trapped again in this plaster cul-de-sac out of which I and my makeshift craft may never escape.*

Ulysses in Hell
A Drama

Le héros a donc cessé d'être un modèle;
il est devenu, pour lui-même
*et pour les autres, un problème.**

[A lawn chair (stage left), on which THE OLD MAN is sitting,
circles slowly on a turntable so that he addresses, alternately,
MY MOTHER AS A YOUNG WOMAN, the audience,
and an unseen chorus of CHILDREN, who sing out the titles of each scene]

Scene 1. ma misi me per l'alto mare aperto

[MY MOTHER AS A YOUNG WOMAN (stage right front
at first, but ambulatory from scene to scene)
begins by addressing the audience:]

On the lawn with his
can of insect repellent,
the mad poet genius.

                                      [THE OLD MAN:]
                        The American artist don't lack talent.

An enormous man, dressed
in khaki shorts, a short-sleeved
yellow shirt, completely
unbuttoned, exposing
a hairy, sunburned chest.

                        What he lacks is chaaaaaracter.

Above the chest, a ragged
red-gold beard half-covering
a weather-beaten face.

                              The malady of the arts is idleness.
Above the beard, twinkling eyes.
                                                           I want
                         to write poetry a man with hair on his chest
                                                       can enjoy.

Disheveled hair that
matches the beard, partly
covered by a cap like those
that tennis players wear.
                                                           I want
                         to find out the known, the unknown and
                                                  the unknowable.

While he talks he pulls
the hairs on his chest or
                                                           I want
                         to put down just where we have got to in
                                                    this year 1952.

fiddles with rubber bands slipped
over the arm of his chair.
                                                           I want
                                      to find my address in time…

…**Scene 12. infin che 'l mar fu sopra noi richiuso**

We continue the conversation
until visiting hours are over.

Then he gathers up all his impedimenta
and lopes across the lawn to doorway.

            [The turntable comes to a stop.
            THE OLD MAN rises from his chair.]

ART is what makes life bearable.

He is an old man by most standards,
but he has great energy and vigor.
He is tall and husky, not fat,
and he seems to tower over me as I struggle
to keep up with his long, loose strides.

Get the good stuff into print.

He has a book he wants me to read,
and so I wait outside his window
until he gets to his room.

*What
is
there*

on the page.

*It's
all
there.*

He lends books to everyone
but must keep a record of who
has what because if one is kept
too long, he asks to have it returned.

*Have you
got that?*

He throws the book down to me,
stands behind the cloudy pane
crisscrossed with wire, gives
a kind of salute, and says, *Ciao*.

[THE YOUNG WOMAN *exits,*
leaving THE OLD MAN *alone on stage.*
He looks out to the audience:]

> *Have you*
> *GOT that?*
>
> *Have you*
> *GOT that?*

[CURTAIN]

*The drama's epigraph is a quote from an essay in Jean-Pierre Vernant's *Mythe et pensée chez les Grecs* (written with Pierre Vidal-Naquet and published in English as *Myth and Tragedy in Ancient Greece*, Janet Lloyd, translator). Vernant writes, "In the very language of tragedy... choral lyric (is) opposed to the dialogue form used by the protagonists of the drama, where the meter is more akin to prose. The heroic figures brought closer by the language of ordinary men not only come to life before the eyes of the spectators but furthermore, through their discussions with the chorus or with one another, they become the subjects of a debate. They are, in a way, under examination before the public. In its songs, the chorus for its part, is less concerned to glorify the exemplary virtues of the hero... than to express anxiety and uncertainties about him. In the new framework of tragic interplay, then, the hero has ceased to be a model. He has become, for himself and for others, a problem."

The material in this poem comes from my mother's unpublished reminiscences of her visits with Ezra Pound at St. Elizabeths Hospital. (I don't make any claims for its historical accuracy; this is his story as I heard it from my mother.) Some of Pound's comments (he would "quote" himself) also appear in his writings. Longfellow's translations of the quotes from Dante sung by the children's chorus read:

  1. "But I put forth on the high open sea" (*Inferno* XXVI. 100)
  12. "Until the sea above us closed again" (142)

Invocation

While still within me
the infant's fetal
heart and mouth pumped
in the mated rhythms
of doomed paramours,
yet because her tongue
struck the flesh anvil
of her tiny thumb,
only her heart's pitched
percussion was caught
on the unravelling
metered paper. As
the monitor scratched
at mechanical verse
with spider-leg pen,
I recognized
on its flickering screen
the ghostly shape
of my mother's jaw
chewing mutely on
unscannable rage
as she floated there
in the amniotic
netherworld of
my ultrasound.

And Anticlea came.

Like that speechless shade
who slipped away with
each embrace, in death
your form evades me.
But when my daughter's tongue

tastes her own mother's blood, and
that first furious wail breaks
the live air, I shall
hear your voice in hers.

BILJANA D. OBRADOVIĆ

A Hierarchy of Names

My nephew says in Italy, where he lives, they call
non-EU people *extracomunitario*, a pejorative word.
In Greece, he introduces himself to Italian tourists, his clients,
as Sean O'Brady, not Dušan Obradović, which is his real name,

and they in turn think of him as an Irishman—a good thing, not a Serb.
When the once US Poet Laureate, Charles Simic came to the US, he
changed his name from Dušan to Charles and removed the funny mark
    on the c.
When a family with my last name came through Ellis Island

on their way to Omaha, Nebraska, at the turn of
the twentieth century they changed their name to O'Bradovich,
making it more Irish, which must have been what the officers pre-
    sumed it was
because of the masses of starving Irish people emigrating to America.

I didn't want to change my name when I became a citizen.
But I often wonder if I should have taken my husband's name
and become Billie Ann O'Gery (or taken his old name Dougherty),
become Billie Ann O'Dougherty, very Irish, very American.

But, I'd need to keep the O as a memory of what used to be there,
what used to be my name before I was urged to assimilate
or be constantly looked down upon as a foreigner.
In a drawer in my office I keep cutouts from envelopes or letters

addressed to me with my misspelled name. It happens all the time.
I am quite surprised at all the possibilities for misspellings,
and now even get excited at the prospect of yet another one, like:
Obradovie, O'Bradovic, or Biljara, Bilhana, Bilzanan or Bityana.

I did not add my husband's name to mine, nor did I add
an h to the end of my last name to make it more American.
Let people struggle, keep asking how to spell it, how to pronounce it.
Perhaps my name will become memorable and one day they will all

know how to spell my name and I won't have to do anything anymore
    about it.
Perhaps they will want to name their children after me one day, or not.
Transform, blend in—is the last thing I want to do.
I don't mind being different, standing out, being weird, just being myself.

Unlike My Happy Baby
after Van Gogh's, *The Baby Marcelle Roulin*, 1888

Don't know if it's a boy or a girl at first glance.
The baby is dressed in a white outfit, with a white cap,
but it has a gold bracelet on its right hand
and a ring on its pinky finger with
a salmon-colored coral cameo, a face on the ring
(even though it's a bit too young for a ring).
It has to be a she, but we cannot be sure
as boys do wear rings and bracelets too.

This is a well-fed baby, just like my son
who was huge at birth. Its blue eyes stare at the floor,
not smiling with its bright red lips.
Must have just eaten, and is wondering what's next
on this Earth…. The postman Joseph's daughter, Marcelle,
longs for her dad to come home from doing his rounds
in Arles, their hometown, to play with her.
Until then she must sit here and pose for Uncle Vincent

who is not very funny. Or, in fact, did Vincent paint
her from memory, as what baby would sit without crying
for so long, especially with smelly turpentine
and oil color fumes surrounding it?
The youngest, chubby, pink cheeked child painting
with a great green contrast in the background, is now back in
Amsterdam, Holland, home to Vincent.
She is his unrealized child forever now.

She's Not a Hot Commodity Anymore
after Von Paul Reeve's photo, *Miss Connie Hung* (c. 2015)

A Bollywood movie star in red costume
in the middle of the shoot with full make-up.
Her lips are so dark, with much lipstick, and
heavy eye make-up with fake lashes.

Come closer and you'll see she's unhappy
about something, her hair covered
with her gold trimmed, fancy sari.
She doesn't feel like dancing in the show.

Her lover called, said he is leaving her
for the lead actress, an Indian. Apparently,
she is not pretty enough for him.
She's Vietnamese. What is she doing

in an Indian movie anyway? She doesn't belong.
No wonder he doesn't want her anymore.
Poor Connie, what will she do now?
Revenge? Yes, but how? For now

she will not show the people on the set
she is upset. She will not shed a single tear.
But, if you come up close, you'll see
the image is not quite in focus and that her

eyes are a little bit wet. Perhaps she can't help it
and her eyes have shed a tear. She is staring
into space, thinking how it could have been,
but it is too late now. Revenge is pointless.

It's better to hide, wear a mask, than be hurt
even more. She will be pushed aside, will have
to deal with it on her own somehow, and find
real friends who will understand how she feels.

Mercury, "Friendship 7"
in memoriam John H. Glenn, Jr. (1921-2016)

The year after my birth, John Glenn
orbited the Earth three times in
some five hours. Too valuable then,
first American to orbit Earth, as if a has-been,
he was suddenly retired, only three years
later, became a senator from Ohio to
serve his country for twenty-four years,
then broke another record too,
as the oldest man to fly in space at 77
years old, as a Discovery crew member.
As a hobby he collected sunsets, as if heaven,
loved watching them from space, remembering still.
Fearless, quiet man, stayed away
from cameras, the glitz, preferred sun's rays.

MATTHEW PORTO

A Whiff of Ambrosia

I.

There was no prayer in the garden.
No one fingered beads, no lips moved.
In one corner, a statue of Aphrodite;
no sparrows at her feet,
only kitschy ceramics.
The enamel beside the stone
proclaimed her mute presence.
The sunlight rose on her neck.

I heard from inside our house
the first strains of a Mahler lied:
Sie hat so lange nichts von mir vernommen,
this love. It was time I rubbed lavender
on my hands, picked a fragrant rose,
dropped it at the statue's feet, and knelt.

II.

And then I saw into the sway of things.
The branches of the myrtle overhead;
the ivy spreading to the steel fence, climbing
her rain-worn, frost-stroked feet;
my suppliant knees were held in its grip
as our identities knit:
I was Adonis, for a moment.
I was the mortal son of Anchises.

But it was by her gait that her son
knew her, even in disguise. Her stride

gave it away when the hitched skirt
dropped: what chance did I,
a desperate husband, have with cold stone?
I noticed the rose still in my hand, and let it fall.

III.

Somewhere behind me
the song reached a crescendo:
Ich leb' allein, the man sang,
and I almost believed it. Then I turned,
saw my wife through the window,
writing something at her desk.
In meinem Himmel, she mouthed
in silence, *in meinem Lieben*.

My knees ached. I stood, brushed off burrs and soil.
As I moved toward the house, a sparrow
beside the lavender jittered
and flew off. I swear
I smelled ambrosia on her nape
when I bent to kiss it.

Way Station: Last Soirée

The sequins on her dress fleck and smile
among the flower-patterned frost on the window.
The chandelier blinks as she crosses the rug.

Outside, snow throttles the black street—
shadows of limbs rake and shift
in the tent of quarter-light pitched by the street lamps.

She moves with an aged cat's gait toward the door.
Voices from the ballroom pad into silence.

The chandelier creaks. Beside the coat rack
she plucks a faux-fur-trimmed scarf
and tucks her fingers in its folds.

Vestibule: the front door peels open;
a car growls at the curb.
In the driver's seat, Charon turns and snickers.
She would swear his breath was perfumed:
rosewood, amber, vetiver, bourbon.

The shadows of thin limbs
rake the light into little knots.
The street lamps wink, then go out.

MICHELE REESE

The Great French Wine Blight

Pale yellow aphids on cuttings
from American grapevines cruised
by steamship, took root ruining
the prized *vitis vinifera*.

Growers set trunks and leaves ablaze
with chemicals, let loose chickens
to peck and feast, flooded vineyards
to drown pests lacing vine supports

of no avail. French wine needed
dense Texas rootstalk to endure
the wingless creatures. We resist
miscegenation or survive.

Crop Insurance

After the lake unfreezes, gnarled cordons
trained on trellises have to be pruned.
A year's growth cut back. Canes contained.
where the wood has died, a sucker lifted
from the roots, tied to wire to begin again.
The loss will be felt come fall. Whole acres
of Cabernet Franc and Pinot Gris succumbed
to winter. There is nothing to do
but submit a claim, order new plants,
wait three years, defend the vineyard from pests,
especially birds. Come fall robins
are the first ones in. They become accustomed
to cannon sounds and inflatable sky puppet
antics. Come fall town will still smell like jelly.

Garnishes

A green acre so selfish and so pure & so enlivened
—Gertrude Stein

On an early morning layover,
I looked around the airport bar
at a sea of Bloody Mary.
I lifted my glass,
tasted vegetables—
tomato, potato, pepper,
onion, garlic, even tamarind
and horseradish.

My palate settled
into conversation
with the stranger next to me.
I swirled a leafy stalk of celery
in the milky red drink, fell into
the routine air-travel patter
and crunches.

Celery tastes tastes . . . like rain
on the fields that we passed over.

Embellishments discarded
on our cocktail napkins.

Grape Pickers

Grandma Mary remembers
school pausing for the harvest,
women and children
among the trellises
filling baskets with deep purple
Concords, bonneted Welch girls
in long white skirts arriving
to help clear the acreage,
ladder boys, and Juan,
her boyfriend in 6th grade.

A yellowed newspaper story
shows her father's harvester
towering over a row.
Its mechanical fingers rip
ripe fruit from the vine
onto its conveyor belts.

Her husband rides
in an air-conditioned cab
over two-acres of grapes
every hour.

RON SMITH

Master

    Sir: With this Letter comes a Negro (Tom)
which I beg the favour of you to sell,
        in any of the islands you may go to,
    for whatever he will fetch,
& bring me in return for him
          One Hdh of best Molasses
    One Ditto of best rum
        One barrl of Lymes—if good and Cheap
  One Pot of Tamarinds—contg about 10 lbs.
Two small Do of mixed Sweetmeats—abt. 5 lbs. each.
    And the residue, much or little,
        in good old Spirits. That this fellow

    is both a Rogue & Runaway
(tho. he was by no means remarkable for the former,
    and never practiced the latter till of late)
I shall not pretend to deny—But he is
    exceedingly healthy,
     strong, and good at the Hoe, the whole
         neighborhood can testifie . . .
which gives me reason to hope he may,
          with your good management,
  sell well, if kept clean & trim'd up
     a little when offerd to Sale.

    I shall very chearfully
allow you the customary Commissions on this affair,
    and must beg the favour of you
        (lest he shoud attempt his escape)
    to keep him handcuffd
till you get to Sea—or in the Bay—

                    after which I doubt not but you may
make him very useful to you. I wish you a pleasant
                    and prosperous Passage,
        and a safe & speedy return,
                            being sir, Yr Very Hble Sert
                            Go: Washington

[RON SMITH'S NOTE: This found poem is taken from a letter by George Washington that can be located online at https://founders.archives.gov/documents/washington/02-07-02-0300, as well as in Henry Wiengek's *An Imperfect God: George Washington, His Slaves, and The Creation Of America*, Farrar, Straux and Giroux (2003) and Sebastian De Grazia's *A Country with No Name: Tales from the Constitution*, Vintage (1999).]

The Berth of Modern Poetry
(at rest in a murky afterlife)

EP

Can you believe Willyum the Wumpus
put up with me sixty years? Never'll
have another friend like him. Cautious, cagey,
good listener. But got so stuck in Amygism
I couldn't yank him out of her huge
tight ass. In fairness, he *tried* to bow-wow
the Big One. But that *Paterson*, big a mess
as my *Cantos*—shorter, sure, but still a big
mess.

     We were on the Penn fencing team
together, while all our tastes were keen,
you could say. Fencing made you think
with the other fella's head, feel
the other fella's muscles rippling
toward a specific action. We used épée's,
heavy as they were, none of that flimsy
foil slinging. He was good. I was better,
more aggressive, good at riposte. Boxing, I stunned
ol' Champ once with a sharp counter-punch.
Bill—Bill was polite, even with a sword in his hand.

And now he's gone. "Struck of the blade
that no man parrieth," I said once,
about some guy I made up. They won't let me
keep my fencing things here,
but I've still got 'em,
somewhere.

WCW

Shit, I'm not gone. Sitting right here, wherever the hell
here is. Sure, I remember meeting Ez, the liveliest,
most intelligent, damndest *thing*
I'd ever come across. Talked poetry all night
in the dorm, nearly put my eye out
with his father's walking cane, thinking
that was fencing. I could have spitted him.
Should have. Sombitch thought he'd defeated
the whole fencing team he couldn't make, including
Leonardo Terrone, our coach from It'ly. Ez was
as bad a fencer as he was a dancer, cook, or carpenter.
Madox Ford said he played tennis "like an inebriated
kangaroo," though he was the only one of us
didn't really drink. Tennis didn't look like tennis
when Pound played it. He'd shout "Egad!" and wheeze,
sit down, jump up, jagged and surprising and slap-dash
as his home-made furniture. Ford did extra time jawing
in a Paris chair cause he couldn't get *out* of it!

Paris's where Ez traded lessons with Hemingway,
writing for boxing, boxing for writing, blow for blow.
Wyndam Lewis popped in and found them going at it
(Pound's fencing gear visible in a corner), said Hem
"without undue exertion" repelled one of EP's
"hectic assaults" after which "Pound fell back upon his settee."
1922, the year of litrachur's nuclear atrocities, Hem wrote
that Ez led "wit his chin" and had "the general grace
of a crayfish," whatever that means. That snake
flattered and coddled our wild man till my friend
pulled *in our time* out of him and bullied a publisher
into launching Mister Macho—who then allowed as how
Ez had "developed a terrific wallop" in his private Paris gym.

From the beginning I let him be village explainer
to my village idiot. I had a lot to learn and he to teach
for all his affectations. Wrote to my mother that
Ez was the essence of optimism. Well, wadn't he?
Even in the loony bin he was the same guy
who taught me what poetry could be.
While failing history at Penn, he was making it,
even in drag in Greek drama, heaving massive breasts
in one ecstasy after another. Euripides,
that was. Genius? A genius passed through him—
a *presence*—from time to time.
He was a beautiful cracked pot, vase
splendidly cracked. Wit and profundity,
profundity and wit, with a huge serving
of plain bull shit.

Slow reader, never read the Rooshans, though
he still had opinions. Eliot said he knew
next to nothing about philosophy, theology,
even French literature. How to describe
his intellect? "Desultory," he said more than once.
Anyhow intellect's only a slice, edges in the mind.
And who has a great mind? Not me. "Prose
for the detestable; lyric for the desirable,"
something like that, he said. Eliot? Too great
for his own good, probably. Book worm.
Did he go crazy? He was always
a bit of a nut, a pure product of America,
especially the First Amendment.

Ha! When Joyce asked his opinion about that
Work in Progress, he wrote, "Nothing short
of divine vision or a new cure for the clapp
could possibly be worth all the circumambient
peripherization." Though he helped JJ at first,

in the Bug House (and long before)
he was anti the cult of Sunny Jim.

Whadya think of this:

> There, in the forest of marble,
> the stone trees—out of water—
> the arbours of stone—
> marble leaf, over leaf,
> silver, steel over steel,
> silver beaks rising and crossing,
> prow set against prow,
> stone, ply over ply,
> the gilt beams flare of an evening.

That's the left hook Hemingway could never teach him
with gloves. That's a Venice that can knock you out colder
than the real thing. His name means "help" in Hebrew
and he was that to all of us. Still: *energy.*
Ezra means *energy*
to me.

Curse Tablet

    May the wild-eyed man
who snatched my carry-on
        from the rental car suffer
  exquisite dental pain
as well as self-administered
        feculent catheters for an STD
  contracted after reading
        the handwritten poems
aloud to a bleeding whore
    he picked up next to a garbage bin
on the Via Appia Antica
        near the aeroporto.
  May he mangle even the Italian sonnet
with a tongue afire
        from an abscess on it.

Photos Of The Event

Emily Mitchell Wallace and Gregory M. Harvey at Paterson Falls.
Credit: Biljana D. Obradović

A bird's eye view of the University of Pennsylvania.
Credit: Anderson Araujo

Conference attendees on a bus tour to visit Ezra Pound's childhood homes outside Philadelphia. Credit: Anderson Araujo

David McKnight guiding a tour outside the Philadelphia Museum of Art. Credit: Anderson Araujo

Catherine Paul, Peter Liebregts, Bernard Dew, Christos Hadjiyiannis, and David Cappella at the Philadadelphia Museum of Art.
Credit: Catherine E. Paul

Conference attendees with Benjamin Franklin. Credit: Anderson Araujo

Above:

The Pound family home at 166 Fernbrook Avenue, Wyncote, Pennsylvania.
Credit: Anderson Araujo

Left:

John Gery at H.D.'s gravesite.
Credit: Biljana D. Obradović

POETRY FROM EPIC 2017   99

Left:

Galateia Demetriou outside William Carlos Williams's home in East Rutherford, New Jersey.
Credit: Justin Kishbaugh

Below:

Miho Takahashi and Mark Byron showing off Mark's Orpheus award for the furthest traveled conferece particiant (Sydney, Australia).
Credit: Anderson Araujo

Above:

Mural at the Paterson Falls.
Credit: Justin Kishbaugh

Left:

Ron Bush during
conference discussion.
Credit: Anderson Araujo

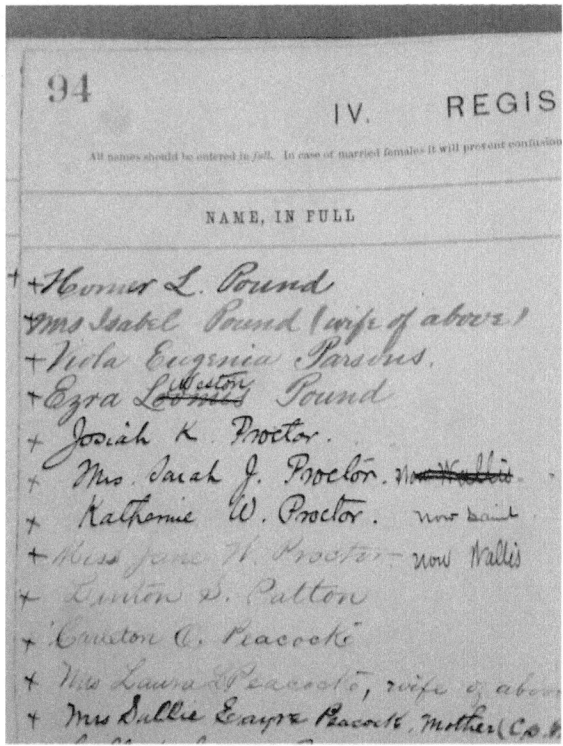

Left:

Homer, Isabel, and Ezra Pound entered in the register of the Calvary Presbyterian Church, Wyncote, Pennsylvania.
Credit: Galateia Demetriou

Below:

Justin Kishbaugh and Catherine Paul opening the poetry reading.
Credit: Anderson Araujo

Above:

Andrei Bronnikov.
Credit: Deric Nugmanov

Right:

Biljana D. Obradović and
Charles Bernstein.
Credit: Anderson Araujo

Left:

Justin Kishbaugh.
Credit: Biljana D. Obradović

Below:

Michele Reese and Biljana D. Obradović
Credit: Biljana D. Obradović

Above:

David Cappella.
Credit: Anderson Araujo

Below:

Mary Maxwell.
Credit: Walter Baumann

Left:

Eloisa Bressan and J. Rhett Forman. Credit: Anderson Araujo

Below:

Rodolfo Brandão de Proença Jaruga. Credit: Biljana D. Obradović

Ron Smith.
Credit: Walter Baumann

Silvia Falsaperla.
Credit: Walter Baumann

Walter Baumann seen through Marcel Duchamp's *The Bridge Stripped Bare by Her Bachelor's Even,* or *The Large Glass.*
Credit: Justin Kishbaugh

Contributors

Charles Bernstein is the author of *Near/Miss* (University of Chicago, Fall, 2018), *Pitch of Poetry* (Chicago, 2016), and *Recalculating* (Chicago, 2013). He is Donald T. Regan Professor of English and Comparative Literature at the University of Pennsylvania, where he is co-director of PennSound. More information at EPC (writing.upenn.edu/epc/authors/bernstein). He won the 2019 Bollingen Prize, first awarded to Pound in 1948."

Born in Italy, transplanted to France, **Eloisa Bressan** has recently moved to the United States, where she is pursuing a doctorate in Comparative Literary Studies at Northwestern University. She holds a B.A. in Classics and a M.A. in Modern Philology from the University of Padua.

Andrei Bronnikov is a Russian poet and philosopher. He is best known for his poetry collections *Zen Elegies* and *Species Evanescens* and is the author of academic papers on Platonism, philosophy of language and mathematics. In 2015–2017, Andrei Bronnikov has completed the first Russian translation of *The Cantos of Ezra Pound*, which was published by the prestigious Nauka publishing house in November 2017 (the volume of 944 pages includes a large biographical article and comments on each Canto—all written by the translator).

David Cappella David Cappella, Professor Emeritus of English and 2017/18 Poet-in-Residence at Central Connecticut State University, has co-authored two widely used poetry textbooks, *Teaching the Art of Poetry: The Moves* and *A Surge of Language: Teaching Poetry Day to Day*. His chapbook, *Gobbo: A Solitaire's Opera*, won the Bright Hill Press Poetry Chapbook Competition in 2006. The complete manuscript has been accepted for publication by Cervena Barva Press in 2019. He recently published a novel, *Kindling*. Currently, he is co-translating *Tracce di un'anima*, the poems of Italian poet Germana Santangelo. Visit his university website: http://webcapp.ccsu.edu/?fsdMember=249.

Mary de Rachewiltz grew up in Gais, Pustertal, in Südtirol. She is the daughter of Ezra Pound and the violinist Olga Rudge. In *Discretions* (1971) she tells her life story up to the return in 1958 of her father to Italy. Among her prolific work from her lifelong dedication to Ezra Pound's poetry and heritage are her Italian translations of a selection of Poundian texts, *Opere scelte* (Mondadori, 1970) and a complete English/Italian edition of *The Cantos* (Mondadori, 1985). With A. David Moody and Joanna Moody, she edited *Ezra Pound to His Parents: Letters 1895–1929* (Oxford University Press, 2011). Apart from archival work at the Beinecke at Yale, co-organizing exhibitions of Poundiana, maintaining the Pound archive at her home, Brunnenburg, Merano, Italy, and giving lectures worldwide on her father's work, she also writes poetry in Italian and English. The poems here will appear in a forthcoming volume of her collected poems.

Patrizia de Rachewiltz grew up at Brunnenburg, a castle in the Tyrolean mountains of northern Italy. She was educated there, in Rome (French Baccalaureat), and in Vienna. She has worked as writer, translator and language instructor. She lives in 's-Hertogenbosch, the Netherlands. She has published several volumes of poetry: *My Taishan* (Raffaelli Editore, 2007); *Dear Friends*, with photographs by Lynda Smith (Palisade Press, 2008); *Trespassing* (University of New Orleans Press, 2008); a volume of prose: *Songs of the Peacock* (Paulist Press, 1977); and numerous translations: *Favole*: Fables by e. e. cummings (All'Insegna del Pesce d'Oro, 1975); *Mr. Wind and Madam Rain* by Paul de Musset (Edizioni C'era una volta, 1994); *Pieroing* by Soichi Furuta (Greco & Greco, 1996); *The Wind in the Willows* by Kenneth Grahame (Edizioni C'era una volta, 1997); *Eros Psyche* by Michael Lekakis (Raffaelli Editore, 2007); and *Your Eyes* by Cesare Pavese (Palisade Press, 2009). Besides appearing in Italian, her poetry has been translated into German, French, Serbian, and Spanish, among other languages.

Silvia Falsaperla is a graduate of the University of Toronto. She lived in Florence for over 10 years where she worked for a literary agency and later as an English teacher, translator and travel journalist. She is an English-language professional and freelance copy editor in Toronto.

She has published short fiction in Canadian literary magazines and her poems have appeared in the AICW newsletters and recently anthologized in *An Anthology of Canadian Writing* published by Longbridge Books, 2018. She is currently working on her first collection of poetry.

J. Rhett Forman is the Director of General Studies and an Instructor of English at Tarleton State University in Stephenville, Texas. He received his Ph.D. and M.A. from the University of Dallas and his B.A. from St. John's College, Santa Fe. He is an alumnus of the University of New Orleans Ezra Pound Center for Literature at Brunnenburg Castle, Italy, and the series editor of "Kulchural Affairs" for *Make It New* magazine. His work has appeared in various publications including *Deep South Magazine*, *Ramify*, *Contemporary Studies in Modernism*, *Borderlands*, *The Common Language Project*, and *A Packet of Poems for Ezra Pound*.

John Gery's seven books of poetry include *The Enemies of Leisure*, *Davenport's Version*, *A Gallery of Ghosts*, and *Have at You Now!* He has also published criticism on a range of modernist and contemporary poets, as well as the book, *Nuclear Annihilation and Contemporary American Poetry: Ways of Nothingness*. With Rosella Mamoli Zorzi and others, he co-authored a walking guide to Ezra Pound's Venice, and with Vahe Baladouni, he wrote a biography of Armenian poet Hmayeak Shems. He has also edited four books of poetry and criticism. Gery has received fellowships from the NEA, the Fulbright Foundation, and the Louisiana Division of the Arts, among others. A Research Professor of English at the University of New Orleans, he directs the Ezra Pound Center for Literature (EPCL), Brunnenburg, Italy. He also serves as Secretary of the Ezra Pound International Conference and is Series Editor for the EPCL Book Series at Clemson University Press.

Jeff Grieneisen, professor of literature and creative writing at State College of Florida, published his first book of poetry, *Good Sumacs*, with MAMMOTH Books and a second manuscript, tentatively titled "Body" is under consideration with another publisher. He was co-founder, and, for 13 years, associate editor of *Florida English*, an annual literary journal that also published special issues of Imagist Conference proceedings. He has placed poetry in a number of journals and anthologies and has published criticism on Edgar Allan Poe and Ezra Pound. He has been invited to present poetry and criticism throughout the U.S. as well as London, Paris, Venice, Edinburgh, and South Tyrol. He divides his time between southwest Florida and western Pennsylvania.

Thomas Heffernan, as recipient of a Research Studentship at the University of Manchester, received an M.A. degree for his thesis "A City of Universals: Siena in the Cantos of Ezra Pound," whose themes of good vs bad government and concern for responsible economic policy, Pound's uses of imagery, monologue, voice are reflected in the present selection. Heffernan has taught at universities in England, the United States, and for many years in Japan, where he developed interest in haiku. His doctorate in English Literature from Jochi Daigaku, Tokyo, was for work on seventeenth-century emblems. Recently, he has taught at St Andrews University and UNC-Pembroke, in North Carolina.

Rodolfo Brandão de Proença Jaruga is a Brazilian lawyer and poet. Born in 1982 in the city of Curitiba, where he lives, he also studied Classical Literature and Philosophy. In 2010 he received a national award for the poetic work "The Ruins of Troy." He is now preparing a new translation of Ezra Pound's *Cantos* into Portuguese.

Justin Kishbaugh is the Associate Director of Academic Success and a Professor of Writing at Roger Williams University School of Law in Bristol, RI. He earned an M.F.A. in Creative Writing from the Jack Kerouac School of Disembodied Poetics at Naropa University and a Ph.D. in English Literature from Duquesne University. His chapbook, *For the Blue Flash*, appeared in 2012, and he is a fan of the Rolling Stones, new sneakers, and his cat, Weapon X.

Mary Maxwell is the author of five volumes of poetry, *An Imaginary Hellas, Emporia, Cultural Tourism, Nine Over Sixes,* and *Oral Lake* (all published by LongNookBooks). Her poetic drama, *Ulysses in Hell*, based on her mother's visits to Ezra Pound at St. Elizabeths, was a finalist for The Paris Review Prize. A winner of the 1990 "Discovery"/

The Nation Award, she has been the recipient of a residential fellowship from the Camargo Foundation in Cassis, France. She has also been a visiting artist at the American Academy in Rome.

Biljana D. Obradović, a Serbian-American poet, Professor of English, Head, Department of English, Xavier University of Louisiana, has published four collections of poems, most recently *Incognito* (Cincinnati: WordTech Press, 2017), translations (Milanović, Gery, Kunitz, de Rachewiltz, Weigl, Osundare), and an anthology of poems, *Cat Painters: An Anthology of Contemporary Serbian Poetry* (New Orleans: Dialogos Press, 2016).

Catherine E. Paul is Professor Emerita of English at Clemson University. She is author of *Fascist Directive: Ezra Pound and Italian Cultural Nationalism*, and with Margaret Mills Harper, the editor of *W. B. Yeats's A Vision: The Original 1925 Version* and *A Vision: The Revised 1937 Version*. She is now a textile and mixed-media artist at the Greenville Center for Creative Arts.

Matthew Porto holds an M.F.A. in poetry from Boston University. His poetry has appeared or is forthcoming in *Salamander*, *The Cresset*, and *Crosswinds*, among others. He is currently pursuing a Ph.D. in creative writing at Texas Tech University.

Michele Reese is a Professor of English at the University of South Carolina Sumter. She published a collection of poems, *Following Phia*, and her poetry has appeared in *Crack the Spine Literary Magazine*, *Ithaca Lit*, *The Paris Review*, as well as other journals and anthologies.

Ron Smith, Poet Laureate of Virginia 2014–2016, is the author of *Humility of the Brutes*, *Its Ghostly Workshop*, and *Moon Road* from Louisiana State University Press. He is also the author of *Running Again in Hollywood Cemetery*, judged "a close runner-up" for the National Poetry Series Open Competition by Margaret Atwood, and subsequently published by University Presses of Florida. He has read his poems about Thomas Jefferson and George Washington at Monticello and Mount Vernon, poems about Virginia history and landscape in the Virginia Senate and House of Delegates, poems set in Rome at the Keats-Shelley House and the U.S. Ambassador's Official Residence in Rome (2017), and poems for the International Hemingway Conference (2018) on the Eiffel Tower and at the American Library in Paris, where he was the Featured Poet. He is Poetry Editor for *Aethlon: The Journal of Sport Literature* and Writer-in-Residence at St. Christopher's School in Richmond, Virginia.

Acknowledgments

Andrei Bronnikov: "Zen Elegies" is excerpted from *Zen Elegies* (Reflections, 2010). © 2010 by Andrei Bronnikov.

John Gery: "Descant on Pennsylvania" originally appeared in *Apiary* (online): http://www.apiarymagazine.com/archive/the-archive/authors/john-gery. Copyright © 2015 by *Apiary* Magazine.

Thomas Heffernan: "Lines Written on Sept. 4, 2011" originally appeared on the North Carolina Arts Council website on the tenth anniversary of 9/11. It also appears in the 2018 annual *Saint Andrews Review*. "Adam's Eve" was first published in the annual *Cairn 49: St. Andrews Review* (2014) and later included in *Five Poems, Fourteen Haiku & One Essay* (St. Andrews University Press, 2015) and the *Ghazal Page* website (2016). "Translator," "Banker, Banking," "A Different Banker," "Billionaire," "A Different Billionaire," and "Pilot" appeared in *Working Voices* (St. Andrews University Press, 2016). "A Haibun" is excerpted from "From a Prefecture in the Deep South" in Thomas Carroll Heffernan, *Christmas Gifts in South Japan: Haiku Essays* (St. Andrews Press, 2003).

www.ingramcontent.com/pod-product-compliance
Lightning Source LLC
Chambersburg PA
CBHW020358170426
43200CB00005B/216